INDEX

STRANGE STONES ON GRIME MOOR

Are the peculiarly named 'bridestones' to do with ancient fertility rites? Or simply a derivation of the Norse work 'Brinkstones'? Or are they really connected with a young man and his future bride? You can judge for yourself as you walk past these huge stones on Grime Moor in the North York Moors National Park. The National Park covers more than five hundred square miles of moor and valley and attracts thousands of visitors all year round. We leave them all behind though and head for the bizarre bridestones, eroded limestone rocks which jut out of the moor like aliens from another planet. Then after passing close to the odd conical shaped hill of Blakey Topping and the nearby ancient stone circle, we stride out along the 'old wife's way' to visit the historic Saltersgate Inn for a bite to eat and a pint. When suitably nourished it will be time to tackle the traverse of the Hole of Horcum with only ghosts of giants and smugglers for company.

FACT FILE
Distance - 7½ miles (12 km)
Time - 4 hours
Map - OS Landranger 94. OS Outdoor Leisure 27
Start - Lockton, Grid ref. 843899
Terrain - Grassy tracks & forest road
Parking - In Lockton or on the outskirts.
Refreshment - The old smugglers haunt The Saltergate Inn

Your Route

Start in the village of Lockton off the A169 Pickering to Whitby road. Leave the village in an easterly direction towards the A169. At the road junction cross carefully over and take the public footpath straight ahead along the wide farm road. In the valley where the track forks take the public footpath to the right up the hill. At the top bear right then immediately left onto a wide farm road away from the farm. In less than a mile look for the entrance to Low Pasture Farm. Turn right here along the public footpath. Pass through the farm-yard then follow the sign for 'bridestones' along a wide track. Cross the stile at the entrance to Staindale Lodge and soon you pass the lodge on the left. Bear left round the lodge and take the track over the stepping stones across the beck. At the kissing gate turn left almost back on yourself to climb onto Bridestones Moor keeping left at the fork. Soon you arrive at Low Bridestones. The track takes you past the strange stones and across the valley to High Bridestones. Just before you reach High Bridestones take the wide path to the right. When you meet a forest road go left. In about a mile leave the forest road as waymarked to the right over a stile and over a rough patch of land to another forest road. Turn left here and soon over a series of stiles following the Link arrows with views to Blakey Topping on your right. At the concrete road pass over the stile to walk along the track known as 'old wife's way'. After a long pull uphill exit over a stile. In a few yards turn right over a stile along a signed, diverted footpath. The path leads to the Saltersgate Inn for your refreshment. The Inn was used by smugglers years ago. Leave the Inn to walk up the hill. A few yards past the severe left bend turn sharp right along the grass verge then left over a stile to descend into the Hole of Horcum. Head for the deserted house then cross a stile heading slightly left and uphill to a gate and stile into a wood. The wide track climbs high to pass through a gate at the top then in a few yards turn right through an unmarked gate. Keep straight ahead now to a large stile at the other side of the field. Turn left here along the wall side into a valley to exit along a wide, rough track.

Follow the waymarks along obvious tracks eventually arriving at a farm. Pass through the farmyard and exit onto the road along the farm drive. Turn right at the road then in a few yards turn right again at the public footpath sign. Follow this path back to Lockton village and your transport.

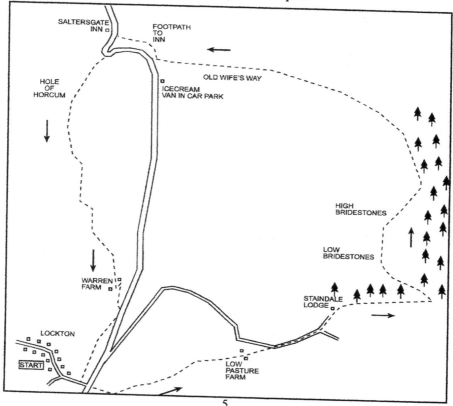

TRAVERSING GLAISDALE RIGG

Glaisdale is without doubt one of the prettiest dales in the North York Moors. To appreciate it fully this walk takes you onto Glaisdale Rigg, with its marker stones, old signpost and iron workings. For a contrast it returns on the opposite side of the dale giving a totally different aspect to this lush, green dale. If you visit Beggars Bridge, a good example of an ancient packhorse bridge, take some of the local butcher's pies with you, they are delicious!

FACT FILE

Distance - 7 miles, 8½ miles if you visit Beggars Bridge
Time - 3 or 4 hours
Map - OS Landranger 94 or OS Outdoor Leisure 27
Start - Glaisdale, grid ref. 775054
Terrain - Moorland bridleways and farm tracks
Parking - Street parking with respect for residents
Refreshments - The Mitre Tavern. Frosts Butchers for delicious pies. Both are in Glaisdale. The Anglers Rest, The Arncliffe Arms and Railway Station Tea Rooms are on the way to Beggars Bridge

Your Route

Leave Glaisdale in a westerly direction towards Lealholm. On the edge of the village at High Leas Farm turn left onto a wide bridleway. This takes you through a gate and climbs onto Glaisdale Moor. Keep straight on at all times to eventually meet a wide farm track. Turn right here then in about fifty yards turn left onto a bridleway. The track falls downhill soon and when you meet a wide track go right to climb up again onto the moor. When the track forks keep right. At the top of the hill you meet another wide track, turn left onto it then shortly right at a junction of wide tracks. This climbs over Glaisdale Rigg to meet a road. Turn left, then immediately left again onto a bridleway through the heather to soon meet a wide track. Cross the track to follow the bridleway opposite then down the hill to exit onto the road in the dale bottom. Turn left here, then at the entrance to Plum Tree Farm turn right along the farm driveway signed as a bridleway.

Go straight on through the farmyard, through a gate and onto a wide track. Soon bear left across a pretty bridge then follow the blue waymarks passing over stiles and through gates which should all be waymarked. Soon you meet the road at a farm entrance. Go left along the road and in about half a mile at the entrance to Bank House Farm turn right onto the farm track at the bridle-way sign. At the farm take the blue waymark to the right through the farmyard and exit through a small gate. Follow the blue waymarks which lead into a copse. Exit from the copse into a field, then through a gate. Keep straight ahead now to the opposite hedge choosing your way through it then head slightly left towards a large building.

Go through the gate then left downhill to a bridleway signpost. Go right here to a gate. Do not go through the gate but turn right towards the oak tree then left through a small gate. Down to the river now and over a bridge then through a gate and onto a paved track. Left at the end as waymarked then follow the signs along a wide track, across a field and eventually to the road. Turn right to return to Glaisdale village. To visit Beggars Bridge pass through the village towards Egton passing pubs and the Station Tea Rooms. When the road falls steeply Beggars Bridge is on your right. You must return the same way you came.

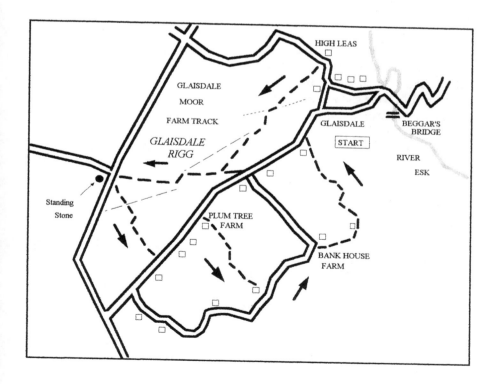

ALONG THE ESK VALLEY

Take a walk onto the wild moors above Goathland then descend to the peace and tranquillity of the Esk Valley. Take a rest at an interesting old pub or marvel at the bouncing waters of the Murk Esk. The spectacular views are free.

FACT FILE

Distance - 8 miles (13km)
Time - 3½ hours
Map - OS Landranger 94 or OS Outdoor Leisure 27
Start - Goathland, grid ref. 833013
Terrain - Good moorland paths and old railway track
Parking - Goathland village car park
Refreshment - Plenty of pubs and cafes in Goathland

Your Route

Start from the village car park in Goathland. It is soon full so be early! From the car park walk towards the village following the sign for Railway Station. In a few yards at the road junction turn left at the Whitby signpost. When the road turns acutely right leave it and go straight ahead downhill to the Railway Station. Cross the railway line with care then turn immediately left up the hill towards the moor. Soon you reach Darnholme, descend into the valley but do not cross the river. Bear right at the farm road past the house on the right following the public footpath sign. In a few yards go left, then left again over the bridge following the yellow waymark. The path winds its way up the steep valley side, there is a seat for the weary near the top!

Soon you are on the moor, keep straight ahead for a short way then turn left through a gate with a yellow waymark. Pass through another gate keeping the farm house on your left. Bear right past the farm to a small gate leading onto the moor. Fantastic views present themselves across Goathland towards Wheeldale Moor. Deep in the ravine below you might hear the huffing and puffing of a steam train of the North Yorkshire Moors Railway.

When the path splits take the one on the right alongside the wall. Where the wall ends go left onto a narrow track past a sheepfold. Head diagonally downhill now aiming for the farm in the distance. When approaching the farm take a narrow track to the right and follow a stone wall which is now on the left. Follow the wall away from the farm until you meet a quiet road. Turn right at the road then in half a mile turn left to walk to Green End. At Green End, just a few houses, turn right onto the public bridleway which is signed through a gate and past the farm buildings. Continue ahead over a stile and along a wide track between two hedges. At the fork go right, signed footpath to Grosmont. Continue following the path and occasional waymarks over several stiles and fields eventually arriving at a wood and a bridge.

Cross the stile and bridge into the wood and soon you will come to a paved packhorse track which eventually exits into a field turning sharp left onto a farm road. Keep left at the road along to the river then follow the footpath sign over the bridge across the Murk Esk on the left. Left towards the church now. If you wish to visit Grosmont you must turn right just past the church. If not, continue straight on up the hill then left at the seat signed rail trail and public footpath.

You now wind your way down to the old railway track. Turn right then continue along the track all the way to Beckhole. Leave the track here as signed to visit the Birch Hall Inn or continue straight ahead past Incline Cottage then through the gate on the signed to Goathland. It is a weary slog up the incline where the old railway coaches were winched up to the top. We have to walk! At the top cross the road into a field signed as a public footpath and soon you will exit onto the road and turn right to return to the car park.

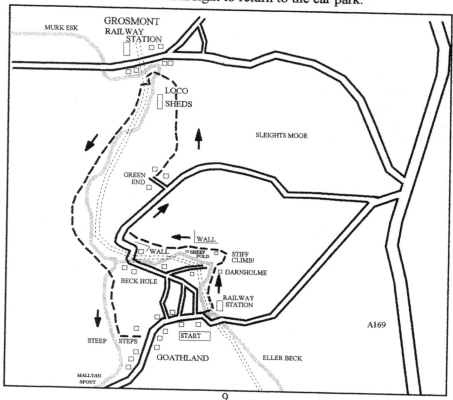

RAPTUROUS RUDLAND RIGG

Dividing the valleys of Bransdale and Farndale is the dominant ridge of Rudland Rigg. The high track over the top of the rigg played its part in the industrial heritage of the area when ironstone mining was prominent. We reach the rigg from Low Mill, a tiny community at the start of the famous daffodil valley of Farndale. This walk links the lush farmland of the sheltered valleys to the bleak nakedness of the rigg with incredible scenery along the way.

FACT FILE

Distance - 12½ miles (20km)
Time - 5 hours
Map - OS Landranger 100 or OS Outdoor Leisure 26
Start - Lowna, grid ref. 686910. Small car park
Terrain - Rough moorland paths and grassy bridleways
Parking - Small area at start
Refreshment - Sandwiches and flask this time!

Your Route

Start from the small car park at Lowna. There is parking here for about eight cars so it pays to be early. Leave on the path at the rear of the car park and soon you will arrive at a footbridge over the River Dove. Turn right over the bridge then left at the sign for Low Mill via Park Farm. Soon, take a detour to the left to visit the Lowna burial ground. It belonged to the Quakers who used this ground between 1657 and 1837.

The track winds its way through the bracken to eventually arrive at a small gate, turn right following the footpath sign and at the bottom of the hill go left at a junction of paths. After struggling through a 'jungle path' you arrive at a small metal gate. Go sharp left here up the hill. At the top of the hill cross the stile on the left. It is a bit tricky now as the path is undefined in the heather, but if you follow in the direction of the arrow and climb the hill diagonally to the right you will meet a fence at the top. If you can't see the next stile follow the fence to the right and you will find it. Cross the stile and the wide track in front of you and continue straight ahead through the heather to meet the road to Park Farm. At the farm pass through the farmyard, the dogs bark but are seemingly friendly! After leaving the farmyard follow the waymark to the left and exit the field by the gate. Continue straight ahead through another gate and soon you will arrive at Cross Farm. Go slightly right here to find a yellow waymark on the farm gate leading to a field. Turn right in the field and look for a stile hidden in the hedge opposite down the hill.

Follow the waymarked stiles down the hill to eventually arrive at a footbridge across the River Dove. Turn sharp left along the river bank after the bridge and after crossing more stiles and another footbridge turn right keeping the river on your right to exit the field by a gate and along a lane to the road. Left at the road then left again at the sign for Low Mill. At Low Mill turn right and in half a mile turn left along the road to Horn End signed as a bridleway to Rudland Rigg. After the farm enter a field, take care there might be the local bull roaming with his concubines around here, and follow the path and way-marks which lead to a footbridge in about half a mile. Cross the bridge and keep to the left following the line of the wall to a stile. Over the stile go diagonally uphill to the right following a worn track which soon bends sharp right and heads ever onwards and upwards through the heather and bracken with confirmation waymarks along the way. When you reach a lonesome tree the path becomes undefined for a few yards. Keep right past the tree and you will soon pick up the path again heading uphill to the left. Climbing now past the shooting butts the path opens out to reach the wide track across Rudland Rigg. Go left here to enjoy the delights of this high rigg walk to the Bransdale road in about three miles. Continue straight ahead towards Gillamoor then in one mile at the start of a steep hill just past the farm turn left at the bridleway sign into a field. Keep to the left here and at the next gate do not pass through but turn sharp right along a wide bridleway. Keep straight on at all times eventually passing through a farmyard to follow the farm drive to the road. Turn left at the road to take you back to the car park at Lowna.

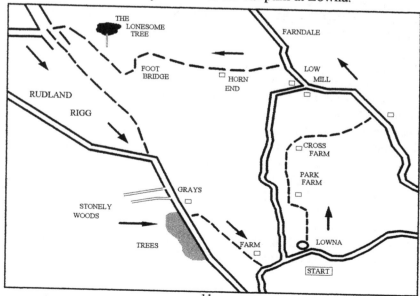

ALONG THE RIVER SEVEN

At Sinnington, there is an interesting church with Saxon and Nor
man features. As we leave the village the route passes the remains of a
12th century Hall used as a barn, then across open fields and through a wood
to the village of Cropton, the birthplace of William Scoresby of Whaling fame.
There are the remains of an ancient cross in the churchyard inscribed with an
interesting old rhyme. The next village we visit is Appleton le Moor with a
fine French Gothic style church, the pleasant old school buildings with vaulted
roof, spire and turret, and the magnificent hotel which was once the Hall. As
you enter the village look out for one of two crosses. It is Low Cross you will
see, High Cross is further away from the village. The cross is not in the form
of a '+' but a collection of stones which were once claimed to have been used
as the village stocks! When you return to Sinnington look out for the 'dry'
bridge. It is very old and was probably used over a mill leat.

The Facts
Distance - 7½ miles (12 km)
Time - 3½ hours
Map - OS Landranger 100
Start - Sinnington, grid ref. 744858
Terrain - Woodland paths and farm tracks
Parking - Street parking with respect for residents
Refreshment - The Fox & hounds at Sinnington, The
Moors Inn at Appleton le Moor and The New Inn at   Cropton

Your Route
After parking with respect for residents in the village head north on
a narrow road keeping the pretty old school on your left. Shortly turn
right towards the church at the 'No Turning Area' sign. Pass the church, or
visit, then where the road turns sharp right look to the left to see the old Hall,
a fascinating building. Soon you will see a sign for 'Bridleway to Cropton'
along a concrete road then across a field. At the far side of the field turn right
following the blue waymark. Shortly left along the bridleway then in a few
hundred yards go right taking the obvious path into the wood. Where the path
forks always take the right option eventually passing through a couple of small
gates then a large one to cross a field to another gate. Through the gate then
immediately left through another gate at the blue waymark and down the hill.
This path is very wet in winter. Keep straight ahead following the occasional
waymark to meet another track. Turn right here at the blue waymark and 'link'

sign to a stile, keeping on the farm road until you meet the main road. If you wish to visit Cropton, the church and the New Inn turn right up the hill. If not, turn left down the hill towards Rosedale then at the bridge take the road on the left towards Lastingham. In about 1 mile at Lower Askew turn left over the bridge then in a few yards leave the road over the stile on the left at the public footpath sign. Cross two fields, a gate and a stile to reach a wood.

Soon the track splits. Careful now, look out for a wide track in a hollow going uphill to the right. Do not take the path down hill! Cross the fence then head for the gate opposite, keep close to the wall then head straight for the farm. Go through the farm yard to the road and turn left to continue along to a 'T' junction to turn left into the ancient village (mentioned in Domesday Book) of Appleton le Moor. Continue to the end of the village and where the road turns sharp right go straight ahead onto the bridleway along the farm track in front of you. Soon there is a choice of paths. Take the one to the right through the gate and diagonally across the field to a small gate into the woods. Continue through the often boggy wood then through a gate to bear left towards the river then follow the waymark to return to Sinnington village.

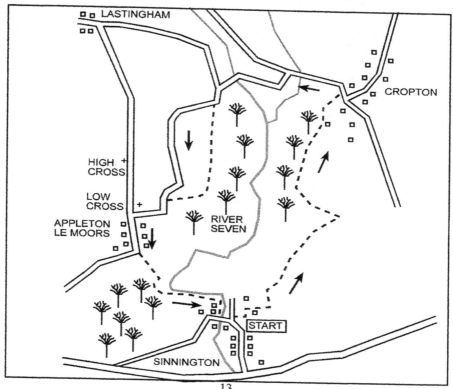

CLIFFS & VALLEYS OF CLEVELAND

S andy beaches, towering cliffs and the site of a Roman Signal Station fea-
ture in this walk along the Cleveland coast. The walk starts in industrial
Cleveland but within a few hundred yards all industry is forgotten as you join
the Cleveland Street, an ancient highway stretching from the Cleveland Hills
to Whitby. Look out on your way for relics of old mines and mining railway
tracks now taken over by weeds and graffiti. More reminders of the county's
industrial heritage can be seen on the high cliffs at Huntcliffe. Unusual metal
sculptures called 'The New Milestones' were commissioned and have been
related to the iron and steel industry. They are to be found close to the Roman
signal station site.

FACT FILE
Distance - 11 miles
Time - 4½ hours
Map - OS Landranger 94, OS Outdoor Leisure 26
Start - Skelton, grid ref. 658189
Terrain - Good field, cliff & woodland
paths
Parking - Car park on Coniston Road
Refreshment - Pubs and cafes in
Saltburn

Your Route
P ark in the small car park at Coniston
Road in Skelton then head off along
the High Street (A173) towards New
Skelton. At the brow of the hill turn right
along Stang Howe Lane which is sign-
posted to Lingdale. In half a mile after
crossing a bridge turn left onto a wide
track which soon narrows and takes you
to North Skelton. Turn right at the road
then after two bridges turn right again
over the cattle grid along a wide public
footpath. At the brow turn left over a stile
at the yellow waymark. Keep straight
ahead to another stile then to a stream and
another stile. Cross the bridge then over

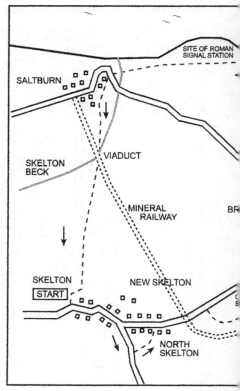

the fields to two more stiles past the old Lumpsey Mine. Cross the mineral railway line then cross a disused railway track keeping straight ahead up the slope to reach a wooden stile. Follow the hedge first round to the left then to the right following the line of the electric poles. At the road keep straight on over the stile then across the field to another stile. Cross another road then over a stile into the field. Keep the hedge on the right and eventually turn through it over a stile, now the hedge is on your left. Continue straight ahead in line with the electricity poles then drop down through a field exiting on a narrow path past the allotments into Carlin How. Cross the road at the pub and head for the main road and pedestrian crossing in front of you. Cross the road and turn right then immediately left and almost immediately right downhill along a wide track with a yellow waymark. In 100yds leave the wide track and keep straight ahead over the bridge. At the road go left and continue all the way to the beach. Turn left here following the signs for the Cleveland Way along the beach and after passing under a pier bear slightly left to climb steadily onto the cliff top. Along the cliffs watch out for the ruined mining fan house, the New Milestone sculptures and the plaque for the Roman Signal

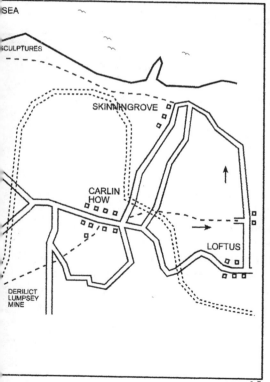

Station. In three miles you arrive at Saltburn. Follow the road along past the Spa then as it bends to the right keep straight ahead onto a smaller road. After passing the children's playground turn left down the steps to meet a path. Turn right here following the Cleveland Way sign. Follow the Cleveland Way signs now but where the path forks go right then at the junction go left. At the bottom of the hill turn right passing the old water mill built in 1649. Keep straight ahead passing under a magnificent viaduct built in the 1870's then leave the river to climb up steep steps into a field. Keep straight on through several gates then go diagonally right towards the housing estate. Continue along to meet Ullswater Drive bearing right, then go left to return to the car park at Skelton.

CAPTAIN COOK COUNTRY

The people of North Yorkshire and Cleveland are proud of their seafaring history so let us walk onto the Cleveland hills to visit a monument to a great seafarer, Captain James Cook. As a young man he spent his early years in North Yorkshire and Cleveland. He went to school in Great Ayton, the old schoolroom is now the Captain Cook Museum. In memory of his great achievements a Whitby banker erected a 60 foot obelisk in 1827 on the edge of the Cleveland Hills from where you can view the Pennines, Durham and the Tees. The walk is only short but is quite strenuous climbing vertically to the monument before heading downhill across to Roseberry Topping only to climb up again over the summit of this most unusually shaped hill.

FACT FILE

Distance - 6 miles/9.6km

Time - 3 hours

Maps - OS Landranger 93 or OS Outdoor Leisure 26

Start - Great Ayton Station, grid ref. 574108.

Parking - There is plenty of room at Great Ayton Station. Alternatively, why not catch the train?

Public Toilets - Nearest public toilets are one mile away in Great Ayton

Terrain - Mainly good paths but some very steep climbs which are slippery in wet weather

Refreshments - Nothing on route but Great Ayton is just one mile away

Your Route

Leave the railway station then turn right over the bridge. Walk for a few hundred yards then turn right at the crossroad by the two white houses. Continue along the road until it becomes a track and starts to climb, passing through a gate. Still climbing the track becomes open pasture.

Keep climbing then follow the wall round to the left towards a gate into the forest. Through the gate bear right following the yellow mark on the tree. Climb up until you meet a track. Cross straight across here and continue to climb. Yes, it is steep! It is a hard, long climb to the top but well worth it if you survive! At the top bear right through the heather to Captain Cook's Monument. Remember where you came in because you must leave by turning left through a path through the heather which soon opens out into a wide, well maintained path for the Cleveland Way. Do not take the path through the stone wall! At the bottom of the hill exit by a gate then cross diagonally right to turn left up the steep, stepped path of the Cleveland Way. Be careful not take the adjacent bridleway! Another stiff climb now onto Great Ayton Moor then follow the line of the wall past the trees in the distance. In a little more than a mile where the trees end, turn left and head for a small gate. Pass through the gate then go down hill on the stone path. You now have a choice of routes. You can either ascend Roseberry Topping which I recommend, or take the easy way out and turn left through the large gate on the left at the base of Roseberry. If you choose the gate continue along straight ahead across the field to join a farm road at another gate/stile. If you climb Roseberry Topping take the rough exit path on the left down the hillside. It is quite arduous but soon ends at a small gate. Keep straight ahead through the gate to meet the same farm track and gate/stile as in the first option. Pass over the stile and keep on to Aireyholme Farm passing in front of the farm to exit onto the road. At the 'T' junction turn right and in a few hundred yards you are back at Great Ayton Station.

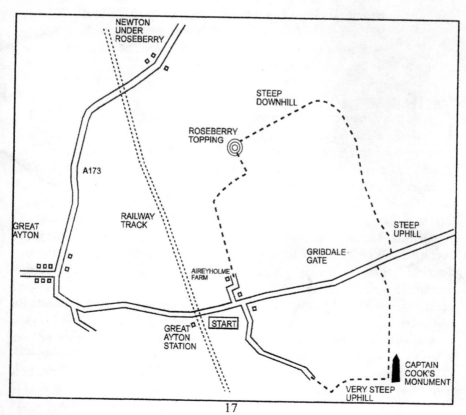

IN SEARCH OF THE GYTRASH

F ind the secret of Julian Park and admire the three waterfalls of Goathland. This walk seems to have everything. Babbling streams, tumbling water-falls, delightful woodland and a mysterious tale. Beware when approaching Julian Park as legend says that a fierce Gytrash (huge dog/goat like creature sent from the devil) roamed these parts and tore the throat out of anything that moved! Move quickly on then and enjoy the three waterfalls along the way and perhaps stop for a sandwich by the side of West Beck as it bounces its way through Scar Wood, but keep a wary eye out for the Gytrash!

FACT FILE

Distance - 8 miles
Time - 3 hours
Map - OS Landranger 94, OS Outdoor Leisure 27
Start/parking - Goathland, village car park grid ref. 833013
Terrain - Good woodland paths and dry farm tracks
Refreshment - Birch Hall Inn, Beck Hole. Several tea rooms and two pubs at Goathland.

Your Route

L eave the village car park turning left past the toilets. In a few yards go left through a gate at the sign for Grosmont Rail Trail. At the end of the field cross the road to continue straight ahead down the old railway incline. This was the route used by George Stephensons railway. I bet they had fun hauling carriages up this incline! Pass incline cottage then if you wish to visit Beck Hole, the Birch Hall Inn and Thomason Foss follow the sign to the right a little way ahead. Thomason Foss is signed from the village near the bridge. If not visiting Beckhole etc., turn left along the signed bridleway into the wood over a stile. Where the path forks go right and climb steadily upwards through the pine forest. At the signpost take the unmarked path to the left, soon it becomes a paved way. Keep straight ahead at the next signpost following the yellow waymark and footpath sign. Still climbing pass through a small gate and soon over a rickety stile into mixed woodland. Exit the wood over a broken stile and keep straight ahead climbing a small hill in front of you. Keep to the wall on the right and eventually exit the field onto a wide track through a gate. Enjoy the superb views from this vantage point. You are now approaching Julian Park, beware of the Gytrash! At the road turn left then in

100 yards turn right along a narrow road to Hollin House Farm. Bear right at the farm then left as directed by the bridleway sign. Pass through two gates at Hazel Head Farm into the farmyard then exit through another gate onto a downhill farm track. Keep on downhill passing through several gates to a stream. Continue straight ahead here crossing the stream on a wide concrete ford. The path continues through two large gates then climbs to meet the road. Go left here and follow the road for about half a mile to a public footpath sign on the left indicating a path through the bracken. At the field go left if you wish to visit Nelly Ayre Foss, our second waterfall, if not continue straight ahead keeping the field on your left. Soon follow the wall on the left to the road. Go left down the hill then at the bridge turn right over a stile onto a path on the bank of West Beck. Follow this path to our third waterfall, the Mallyan Spout. Shortly after the waterfall turn right up the hillside as indicated to return to Goathland. At the road turn left past Prudom House Tea Rooms, or pop in for some refreshment, then go right along a wide, stony path to pass a public footpath sign and the Goathland Exhibition Centre. Soon go through a rusty gate into a field. Continue over three stiles and a footbridge, through a campsite to soonexit onto a wide track. Turn left onto this track to return to Goathland. Left at the road then right to the car park.

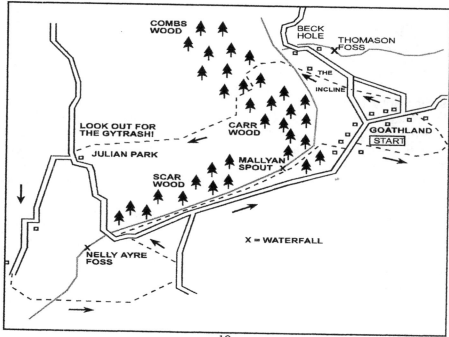

STEAM AND STONE BRIDGES

The puffing of an out of breath steam engine of the North Yorkshire Moors Railway climbing the steep track to Goathland means that we will have some puffing ourselves to do as we walk to Carr End at Glaisdale. The famous Limber Hill stands in our way and the steep footpath past The Delves will test our aerobic efficiency to the full.

FACT FILE

Distance - 11½ miles (18½km)
Time - 4½ hours
Map - OS Landranger 94 or OS Outdoor Leisure 27
Start - Grosmont, grid ref. 826053
Terrain - Mainly good paths with some short, steep climbs
Parking - Two car parks. One at railway station, the other outside the village under the bridge
Refreshment - Glaisdale End Tea Rooms, Postgate Inn Egton Bridge, Hazlewood Tea Rooms at Grosmont and Pub

Your Route

Grosmont is situated at the eastern end of the North Yorkshire Moors Railway. Visit the engine sheds if you have time. Leave the car park towards the railway station and turn right immediately over the level crossing. Cross the bridge over the Murk Esk and take the left fork signed 'Rail Trail' up the hill past the school and church. Through the gate turn right, climb the hill then at the seat turn left at the sign for 'Rail Trail'. The path falls to a cinder track running alongside the railway. Keep on this track eventually crossing a road at the houses to continue along through a gate onto the track again. This is the route of the original railway built by George Stephenson from Whitby to Pickering. In about half a mile at a clearing take the public footpath over a stile on the right into a field, then go immediately left. Follow the river and after passing over two stiles bear slightly right passing some hawthorn shrubs on your left.

Soon you pick up a series of signposts, follow the signposts and waymarks to eventually arrive at a junction of tracks. Take the track to the right signed to Egton along a path through woods. After crossing a couple of footbridges climb up to a ruined building. Go left here towards the house passing it on the left to a footpath sign. It is a long, hard climb through the woods. At the fork go right then right at the footpath sign in a few yards to exit onto the road over a stile. Left now, then in a quarter of a mile follow the bridleway sign on the right climbing onto the moor. Keep to the single track through the heather all the way to the road. Go left, then right at the footpath sign. At the wall go right then follow the wall, then a fence to a pair of gates. Follow the blue waymark and continue along through bracken as the path descends to a farm track and eventually left to a farm. Pass through the farmyard to exit onto the farm drive. When the drive turns right take the wide grassy track on the left, through the gate straight ahead then sharp left down the hill.

Leave the field through a gate to go right along a bridleway past Hall Grange Farm. Soon leave the bridleway at the footpath sign on the left. Keep following the waymarks and eventually start to climb a long hill towards The Delves and a stone stile. At the top of the steep climb turn right to exit onto the road. Right now down the hill, then in about three hundred yards take the path signed 'To Arncliffe Woods' on the left which soon joins an old paved way. The path falls steeply to the River Esk and Carr End, bearing right at the road to Beggar's Bridge, a fine 17th century bridge. Pass by the bridge to soon climb Limber Hill. At the severe bend near the top go right through a gate then in a few yards go left through another gate. Soon join a wider track and continue along over several stiles, fields and through a wood, then another field to exit onto the road turning right to Egton Bridge. At the road junction go left then in a few yards turn right along a permitted path by courtesy of Egton Estates. (If you wish to visit the Postgate Inn ignore this turn and continue under the bridge). At the end of the estate track turn right along the road, over the bridge then straight along the road to Grosmont.

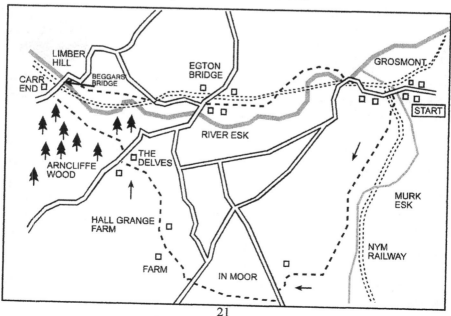

TWO LITTLE KNOWN YORKSHIRE DALES

This woodland walk visits two dales, Ash Dale and Riccall Dale. Although only one mile apart the variation in scenery and vegetation is vast. It is best walked in the spring to appreciate the wild flowers. The North York Moors with its bleak terrain is also host to secluded valleys and griffs. Whilst around its perimeter are interesting market towns. This walk starts in Helmsley, a market town on the southern edge of the moors. It has many fine buildings surrounding the market square and a superb castle which was built around 1200AD on an outcrop of rock.

FACT FILE

Distance - 7½ miles (12km)
Time - 3½ hours
Map - OS Landranger 100 or OS Outdoor Leisure 26
Start - Helmsley, grid ref. 613840
Terrain - Woodland paths and forest road
Parking - Two car parks. One in the market square the other at the castle
Refreshment - There are numerous cafes, pubs and sandwich shops in Helmsley.

Your Route

Leave Helmsley market square past the church turning right along the road which runs between the church and the pub. Turn right at the top and in a few yards turn left into Warwick Place then follow the 'link' sign to Carlton. The link is the missing link offering a fifty mile return route for walkers having completed the ninety three mile Cleveland Way from Helmsley to Filey Brigg.

When the road ends take the narrow path straight ahead past the cemetery and cricket field. Follow waymarks now for 'link' as the path skirts round fields to eventually enter Ash Dale through a gate. Ash Dale is a narrow, steep sided dale and can be muddy if wet. If you are walking in early summer your nostrils will be filled with the smell of wild garlic. Keep onward and upward through the dale eventually arriving at a junction of tracks. Take the track to the right here signed 'Link Carlton ½ mile'. At the road turn left. In half a mile turn right in the direction of the sign for 'Link Beadlam Rigg 2 miles'. Follow the blue bridleway arrow straight ahead up a track opposite. Do not walk along the concrete road. Where the track splits bear left at the 'link' sign keeping to the fence on your left. Enter the wood then in about 200yards turn right down a steep narrow track through the wood at the 'link' sign. Cross the wide farm road and take the track straight ahead down towards the stream. When the 'link' route goes left through a gate you must turn right to leave the 'link' route., turning right along a wide track which soon opens out into a field. Where the track forks keep right and soon join a wide forest road. Go left here then in a little over a mile at the top of the hill take the right fork up a seriously steep forest road. At the top of the hill bear left then through a gate into a field. Keep straight ahead along an obvious farm road soon passing some barns and an old farmhouse. When the road turns sharp right and leaves the wood turn left to enter a wood at a clearing. Keep close to a fence on your right and a path soon becomes obvious. When the trees end the path enters a field through a gate on the right and eventually exits onto the farm road at Rea Garth Farm. Cross the road and aim for a farm gate into a field. Through the gate keep straight ahead to the left of the trees and soon you will see yellow waymarks to guide you back to Helmsley. At the road turn left then right at the junction to return to the market square.

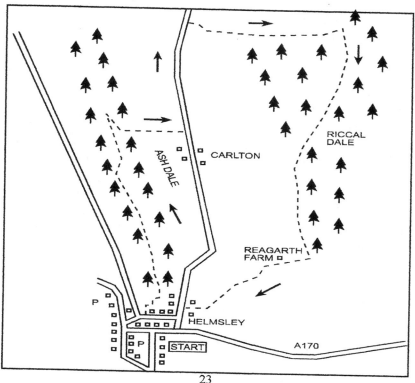

A 2 DAY TWELVE MOOR HIKE
DAY 1 - RAVENSCAR TO GOATHLAND

This route was devised for the walker who would like to make a weekend of hiking across the North York Moors. Apart from the odd exception the route keeps mainly to the high open moors. It would be wise to walk the route in summer to enjoy the heather and avoid the bogs! It passes by streams, waterfalls, a superb cross and a couple of not so superb ones! The views are excellent from Simon Howe, Lilla Cross, Goathland Moor and the start/finish at Ravenscar. Please go well prepared as there is no chance of refreshment along the way. If you prefer a one day hike you could arrange transport to pick you up at Ravenscar or Goathland.

FOR FACT FILE SEE PAGE 26
FOR MAP SEE PAGE 27

Your Route. Day 1 - 15 miles

The route begins at Ravenscar which is on the coast between Scarborough and Whitby. There is ample roadside parking here. Start with the Raven Hall Hotel at your back and walk uphill along the road you arrived on for about a quarter of a mile then turn right at the bridleway sign along Robin Hood Lane. Keep straight ahead at the end of the road up a rough track following the bridleway sign.

When the track forks go left and follow the yellow arrow to the road and the radio mast. Turn right here at the bridleway sign onto a wide track across the moor. In one mile the track splits, take the bridleway marked with a blue arrow to the right. Follow this to the farm road then turn left following the sign for bridleway. Shortly you meet the busy main road. Cross with care then follow the public footpath sign onto an old road then over a stile into a meadow. Follow the yellow arrow keeping close to the fence on your right. Eventually the path falls into Wragby Wood to a junction of becks. Follow the path around to the right, when the path splits bear left then right over a wooden bridge. Follow the track to the right and eventually cross the beck continuing straight ahead on the obvious track along the valley. Keep following the beck as it twists and turns along the valley passing the odd stile and the occasional footpath sign. Soon the path crosses Hollin Gill coming in from the left. Ignore the path along the Gill to keep right taking the line of Brown Rigg Beck. The path becomes undefined in places but keep near to the wall on the left, eventually crossing to the other side when a more prominent track becomes visible. Soon you arrive at some shooting huts and a house. Take the path to the right of the huts and join a chalk farm road. Go right here for a few yards then leave the road to the left aiming for the yellow waymark in the corner of the wood. Cross the stile then in a few yards cross a high rise stile. Follow the path around to the left and keep close to the fence as it too eventually swings left which leads to a rickety gate into a wood.

Leave the wood over a stile onto a farm road, go left over the bridge then immediately right onto a narrow path which follows the marshy beck along a wide valley. The path is a struggle at times disappearing into the heather then reappearing when it seems all is lost. Keep to the valley heading west but stay close to the left hillside or you could end up in the bog! After struggling for about a mile you meet a moorland road. Turn right here to a post in the distance. At the post take the path to the left following a trail sign. Enter the wood and go left past the ruins of John Bond's Sheep House. Ignore the path to the right and continue along the line of the fence on your left soon crossing a stile onto the moor. At the Beck keep to the track on the right. Continue along to another Beck crossing, then when the track splits take the wider one to the right. This rough track climbs over Green Swang onto Fylingdales Moor to a signpost near Lilla Cross. Turn right here signed to Goathland and soon right again to a gate. Through the gate go immediately left along a wide bridleway. It's downhill all the way now passing Ann's Cross and York Cross standing proud if a little dilapidated at the side of this rough track. In about three miles cross the A169 and pass through the gate the opposite. A short track takes you to a minor road. Turn left onto the road and in ¾ mile take the public footpath on the right. This is a rough track through the heather sometimes undefined at the start. But head diagonally across the moor aiming for Goathland in the distance and soon you will see a tarn. Pass close to the tarn and pick up the wide track to Goathland Station and Goathland for your overnight stop.

ROUTES 12 & 11
A 2 DAY TWELVE MOOR HIKE
DAY 2 - GOATHLAND TO RAVENSCAR

FACT FILE FOR BOTH DAYS

Distance - 29 miles (47km).

Time - 2 days.

Start - Day 1 - Ravenscar, grid ref. 981016. Day 2 - Goathland, grid ref. 833013

Terrain - Rough & tough over high moorland and a boggy valley.

Maps - OS Landranger 94, OS Outdoor Leisure 27.

Accommodation - B&B is plentiful at Goathland. The camp site is 1 mile along the Pickering road at Brow House Farm. The YHA, Wheeldale Lodge is 2½ miles away near Hunt House and is on route for the second day. Both are signed from the junction near the church.

Your Route - Day 2 - 14 Miles

Start the second day from the War Memorial in the centre of the village and take the road South West towards the Mallyan Spout. Soon you arrive at the Mallyan Hotel. Take the path to the right of the hotel signed to Mallyan Spout. At the bottom of the slope turn left along the riverbank and past the Mallyan Spout, an outstanding waterfall. Follow the Beck south for 1½ miles to the Egton Bridge road. Join the road turning left up the hill. Ignore the bridleway sign on the right but take the public footpath sign to the right a little further along past a house. Continue along the path climbing gently, when the stone wall ends take the track to the left uphill to join the YHA road a little further along.

Turn right onto the road and continue along following the sign for YHA and 'Roman Road via Stepping Stones'. The road soon becomes a track as it passes Hunt House on its way to the Youth Hostel. After passing the YHA the track descends to a bridge over a small stream. Our route goes to the left and uphill over Howl Moor to Simon Howe to follow the final leg of the Lyke Wake Walk route to Ravenscar. The path climbs steeply at first then levels out over the moor until it climbs a little more to reach the Bronze Age Barrow of Simon Howe. Go straight past the Howe, of which there are over 3000 on the North York Moors, and take the wide track straight ahead to descend for 1½ miles to meet the North Yorkshire Moors Railway track (please cross with care) and through the nature reserve of Fen Bog. Soon the path reaches Eller Beck Bridge and the A169. Go left for a few yards to the bridge then turn right along the wide unmade road, over the stile and onto the land belonging to the

Ministry of Defence. When the road ends keep straight ahead close to the boundary fence on your right. Soon the fence swings to the right, ignore this and continue straight on and down to cross Eller Beck in front of you. On the opposite bank you will know detect a well-worn track to Lilla Rigg. Keep on the track until it meets a stony moorland road. Go left here to a 'T' junction. Cross over onto the track opposite through the heather following the yellow arrow. In a few yards you will arrive at Lilla Cross, a memorial to a brave Saxon. In 626AD the red-haired Lilla sacrificed his own life to save that of his king. He was buried on this Howe and the cross erected in his memory. Continue straight ahead past Lilla Cross on a wide track which soon joins another wider track. Bear slightly right here then keep straight on until the track splits. Take the left fork over High Moor passing Burn Howe then in about two miles descend steeply into a lush, green valley. Cross the footbridge over the beck then follow the yellow arrow to the right then round to the left and climb steeply up the end of the rigg. Almost a scramble!

The track joins a concrete disused army road and eventually meets the A171. Cross the busy road with care and continue along the footpath opposite to climb onto Stony Marl Moor and Howdale Moor to aim for the radio mast in the distance. At the mast cross the road and follow the public footpath sign to take you back to Ravenscar.

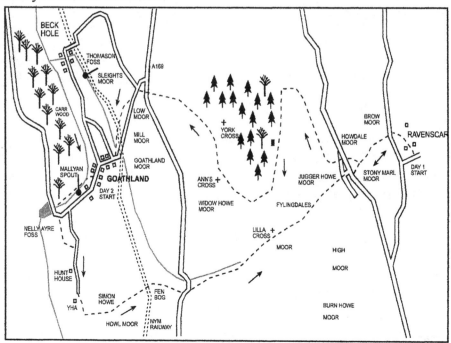

27

OTHER TRAILBLAZER BOOKS

Mountain Biking around North Yorkshire
Mountain Biking The Easy Way
Mountain Biking around the Yorkshire Dales
Mountain Biking around Ryedale, Wydale & North York Moors
Mountain Biking on the Yorkshire Wolds
Beadle's Bash - 100 mile challenge route for Mountain Bikers
Mountain Biking in the Lake District
Mountain Biking for Pleasure

Curious Goings on in Yorkshire

Walking to Crosses on the North York Moors
Short Walks around Yorkshire's Coast & Countryside
Walking to Abbeys, Castles & Churches
Walking on the Yorkshire Coast
Walking the Ridges & Riggs of the North York Moors
Walking around Scarborough, Whitby & Filey
Ten Scenic Walks around Rosedale, Farndale & Hutton le Hole
Twelve Scenic Walks around Ryedale, Pickering & Helmsley
Twelve Scenic Walks around the Yorkshire Dales

The Crucial Guide to the Yorkshire Coast
The Crucial Guide to Ryedale and the North York Moors
The Crucial Guide to the City of York & District
The Crucial Guide to Crosses & Stones on the North York Moors

The MG Log Book
Triumph TR log Book

Available from Book Shops, Tea Shops, Cycle Shops
and
Tourist Information Centres